HERCULES

and Other Tales from GREEK MYTHS

(Authorized Abridgment)

By OLIVIA E. COOLIDGE

Illustrated by David Lockhart

SCHOLASTIC INC.
New York Toronto London Auckland Sydney Tokyo

ISBN 0-590-08542-5

30 29 28 27 26 25 24 23 22 21 20   4 5 6 7 8/8

Printed in the U.S.A.   01

CONTENTS

INTRODUCTION

GREEK LEGENDS have been favorite stories for many centuries. Even though we no longer believe in the Greek gods, we enjoy hearing of them because they appeal to our imagination.

The Greeks thought all forces of nature were spirits, so that the whole earth was filled with gods. Each river, each woodland, each great tree had its own god or nymph. In the woods lived the satyrs, who had pointed ears and shaggy legs of goats. In the sea danced more than three thousand green-haired, white-limbed maidens. In the air rode wind gods, cloud nymphs, and the golden chariot of the sun. All these spirits, like the forces of nature, were beautiful and strong, but sometimes unreliable and unfair. Above all, however, the Greeks felt that they were tremendously interested in mankind.

From very early times the Greeks began to invent stories to account for the change of seasons, the sudden storms, the good and bad fortune of the farmer's year. These tales were spread by travelers from one valley to another. They were put together and altered by poets and musicians, until at last a great body of legends arose from the whole of Greece. These gave a clear picture of the great and lesser gods, and how men should behave to please them.

Ruler of all gods was Zeus. He lived in the clouds with most of the great gods in a palace on the top of Mount Olympus, the tallest mountain in Greece. Lightning was the weapon of Zeus, thunder was the rolling of his chariot, and when he nodded his head, the whole earth shook.

Almost as powerful as Zeus were his two brothers, who did not live on Olympus: Poseidon, ruler of the sea, and Hades, gloomy king of the underworld, where lived the spirits of the dead. Queen of the gods was blue-eyed, majestic Hera. Aphrodite, the laughing, sea-born goddess, was queen of love and most beautiful of all. Apollo and Artemis were twins, god of the sun and goddess of the moon. Apollo was the more important. Every day from dawn to sunset he rode the heavens in a golden chariot. Artemis, the silver moon goddess, was goddess of unmarried girls and a huntress of wild beasts in the mountains.

Gray-eyed Athene was the goddess of wisdom. She was queen of the domestic arts, particularly spinning and weaving.

One more god who lived on Olympus was Hermes, the messenger. He wore golden, winged sandals which carried him dry-shod over sea and land. He darted down from the peaks of Olympus bearing messages from Zeus to men.

The Greeks have left us so many stories about their gods that it hardly would be possible for everyone to know them all. We can still enjoy them because they are good stories. In spite of their great age we can still understand them because they are about nature and about people.

Hercules

I. THE YOUTH OF HERCULES

THE FIRST STORY about Hercules tells of his strength when he was less than a year old. One night his mother, Alcmena, fed him and bathed him as usual. Then she put him to bed for the night with his twin brother, Iphicles, in a cradle made of a great bronze shield which their father, Amphitryon, had won in battle. She kissed the little boys lying close together, and rocked them gently for a time until they fell asleep. Presently she crept away, and soon the whole house lay silent and dark.

Now Zeus was the protector of Hercules. His wife, Hera, was jealous. This night she sent two dark snakes silently sliding across the floor towards the shield. Just as the snakes coiled themselves up to strike, Zeus lit up the whole room with brightness. At the warning the children awoke. When Iphicles saw the swaying heads peering at him over the rim of the shield, he screamed aloud in fright. Not so Hercules; he grasped the snakes by the neck in his fat baby hands and clutched with all his might.

In another moment all the house was in an uproar. The angry snakes whipped back and forth. They wound their coils about the baby's arms and tried to squeeze. But Hercules only gripped tighter and choked them till they were limp and helpless. In the next room, Alcmena leaped from bed, awakened by the brightness, the sounds of struggle, and the screaming of Iphicles.

"Quick!" she gasped to her husband. "Quick! Get your sword!"

Amphitryon jumped up half awake and fumbled for the weapon that hung on a peg beside his bed. At that moment the bright light vanished. They could hear no more struggle—only the sound of Iphicles' crying.

"Lights! Lights!" Amphitryon shouted to his household. "Bring torches, unbolt the doors!"

People flocked into the room, Amphitryon first with his drawn sword in his hand, Alcmena close behind him, and the servants crowding with torches through the door. There in the cradle lay Iphicles, hushed now but white with fear. Beside him lay Hercules chuckling to himself as he held out his arms to his father. In the two tiny fists lay the dead bodies of the snakes, choked by the strength of his grip.

Alcmena picked up Iphicles and comforted him, but Amphitryon merely tucked the blanket in again over Hercules and let him go back to sleep. From that time on both parents knew that this child would be a mighty hero.

The legends say that when Hercules grew to manhood the gods made him bind himself for eight years in the service of King Eurystheus, who ruled over the city of Mycenae.

This king was a weakling and a coward. He was jealous of the great hero and proceeded to give him the hardest tasks he could find. These tasks are generally called "The Twelve Labors of Hercules" and are the most famous of his deeds.

2. THE FIRST TWO LABORS

THE FIRST of the twelve tasks given to Hercules was the killing of the Nemean Lion. This great beast had his lair near the sacred grove of Zeus at Nemea whence he ravaged the nearby countryside. Hercules took the great bow that none but he could bend, and made himself a mighty club from the trunk of an olive tree which he tore up by the roots. With these weapons he went up the valley toward the rocky cleft where the beast was supposed to live. It was noon as Hercules passed through Nemea, finding no track of the monster and hearing no sound of roaring. Though it was midday, the whole place seemed deserted. No man was busy plowing. The cattle strayed in the fields untended while the inhabitants shut themselves up safe indoors. It was better to lose a cow or a sheep than one's own life, and from this beast not even the bravest man was safe.

Hercules passed through the silent valley and began to climb the wooded hill as the sun sank low. Presently he heard a rustling in the undergrowth. He made towards it. As he came out onto a wide clearing, he saw the lion. The lion was not in a warlike mood; it had

4

killed and eaten already and was now going home to sleep. It was an enormous monster. Its great, hairy face was dark with blood and streaked with dust. It padded up the hill, head low, making for its den.

Hercules crouched down behind a group of bushes fitting an arrow to the string. With all his strength he let fly, and his aim was true. The arrow struck the lion full in the side. To the hero's amazement it simply bounded off and fell on the grass. Then Hercules knew that this was no ordinary lion. Before the enraged beast could turn upon him, he shot again. Again he hit. Again the arrow bounded off and was lost. Before he could shoot a third time, the lion was on him with a mighty spring. Hercules met him in mid-air. In his left hand he held his folded cloak hastily flung over his arm to break the force of the blow. With the right he raised his club and struck the lion full on the forehead with such fearful force that the club broke clear in half and he was left defenseless.

The lion dropped to the ground dazed. Were it not for the bush of hair that protected his head, even his huge skull might have been cracked. As it was, he still stood on his four feet but blinded and staggering, shaking his great head slowly to and fro. Then with a quick spring, Hercules was on his back and his arms were

about the lion's throat. In vain did the beast rear up and rend the air with his claws, then drop back and scrape great furrows in the ground. In vain did he dash himself from side to side. The man still clung. The mighty arms gripped ever more tightly round his throat. He opened his mouth to roar, but no sound came forth. He reared up again and this time was held there helpless while his useless forepaws beat the air. At last his struggles grew fainter until finally he went limp. Hercules had strangled him by main strength.

Hercules was immensely proud of his first achievement. He skinned the lion—no easy task to cut off that iron hide—and went back to King Eurystheus with the thing slung about him as a cloak. The two forepaws fastened it about his neck. At will, he could draw up the lion's head over his own. He came swaggering into the presence of Eurystheus. That coward king had hoped to get rid of Hercules and feared that the hero knew it. He was so terrified at the fierce lion's head and the great man who carried it that he turned white and trembled before the eyes of all his court. He quickly left the hall before Hercules could come near him. The bold hero shouted with laughter, while the attendants whispered among themselves.

Eurystheus was furiously angry with Hercules, who had shown him up as a coward in everyone's sight; so the next time he determined to give him a task that he simply could not do. He commanded Hercules to kill the Lernaean Hydra. This was a great swamp serpent with nine heads, one of which was actually immortal. It had such a dreadful poison that it infected the very air. The whole region around it was deserted, for no one dared use the water from the springs near where it dwelt. This time Hercules did not go on his quest alone but took with him Iolaus, son of his twin-brother.

Iolaus was still a boy, and his uncle took him not to help him against the Hydra, but to travel with him and to drive his chariot. The two rode across the deserted country where neither man nor beast could dwell until they came to the springs of the river which welled out beside the Hydra's den.

Here Hercules left Iolaus with the horses and himself stepped forward and sent a few arrows whizzing into the darkness of the cave. He knew from the hissing within that he had roused the animal. As it slithered forward out of the rock, he sprang upon it and dashed his club on the nearest flickering head. The head dropped crushed and shapeless as the long neck went limp, but the beast came coiling forward, eight heads still darting venomously. Hercules gave ground and lifted his club once more. Even as he did so, he saw the limp neck rouse again. From its shattered end grew two new necks, and from each of these a head. Again he swung his club and again jumped back a pace. Once more the same thing happened. The second shattered head grew whole again and became not one head, but two.

Then the hero was desperate. He saw that against this monster even his strength could not prevail alone. "Iolaus!" he shouted, "Iolaus!" not daring to look

round and see whether the boy was still with the horses or whether he had run for his life at the dreadful sight.

"Here I am," called a steady voice from behind him. "Here I am."

"Run! Get a dry branch and light it. Then come here to me," shouted Hercules, giving ground again before the forest of heads. He dared not let the poisonous fangs come too near. "Bring fire to lay across each head as I crush it. We will sear it well and see if it will grow again."

Iolaus tore for the thicket, but he had to light the whole grove to get enough fiery branches. All this took time. Meanwhile Hercules still battered vainly at the mass of heads. Every time he crushed one, two grew up in its place. But the Hydra shrank a little from his blows and for a while he could keep it at bay.

Iolaus rushed up the slope to Hercules with a great branch in his hand which flared up as he came. He was only just in time. Already Hercules' foot was caught fast in the Hydra's coils and the poisonous fangs were darting at his face. But as the hero struck out again, Iolaus with utter fearlessness darted in and laid the burning branch across the crushed and bleeding head. There was a fierce hissing, and the whole Hydra recoiled. At that Hercules wrenched his foot loose and struck again. Once more Iolaus darted in and laid his branch across the shattered neck. So they fought the Hydra together, Hercules dealing the blows and the boy dashing boldly within reach of the poisonous fangs to lay his burning branch across each wound. At the touch of the fire, the heads did not grow again. After long hours they were victorious together against all but the immortal head, which could not die. Finally Hercules cut it off and buried it, still struggling, under a mighty rock. Then he and Iolaus looked down at the monstrous beast.

The Hydra lay there in a huddled tangle of snaky heads. The coils of its vast body trailed limply over the ground. All around the bare, poisoned earth was torn up by the struggle. Great furrows, blackened branches, and traces of blood were everywhere. The hero looked at it for a moment, weary but triumphant; then taking out his arrows he plunged them in the poisonous blood of the beast. He put them back in his quiver, fastening them very carefully. He laid his hand on Iolaus' shoulder and they went down together to look for the horses.

3. THIRD AND FOURTH LABORS

HERCULES again presented himself ready to do whatever King Eurystheus should command him. The King was disappointed that Hercules came back alive. For this time Eurystheus had rather run out of ideas. He would have liked to find something dangerous, but he could only think of something difficult. So he ordered the hero to capture a beautiful deer called the Cerynean Hind. While Hercules performed this labor, which took him a full year, King Eurystheus settled down to think of something really dangerous for next time.

The hind that Hercules was to fetch was a beautiful animal with golden horns, the favorite of Artemis. It ran wild on the wooded hills and shady valleys of Arcadia.

For a whole year Hercules hunted the animal through half the hills of Greece, wishing to take it alive. Though he spread the trails with nets, and though he himself was a tireless runner, he could never catch it. Often on moonlit nights he would see a glint of light on the pale gold horns. Instantly the hind was up and away, swifter even than other deer, leaping obstacles and avoiding nets as though the goddess Ar-

temis were guiding it. Hercules saw that he could never catch the hind unarmed, so he wounded it with an arrow and thus captured it. Slinging it across his shoulders, he began the long journey back in triumph. As he walked, there appeared to him in the woodland a young girl, fairer than human, with white tunic to the knee and bright hair caught back in a band of gold.

"How dared you harm my beautiful hind?" she demanded angrily.

14

Hercules knew he was in the presence of Artemis and he begged her to forgive him. He pleaded the command of Eurystheus and promised that after he had shown it to the king, the beast should be let go. Presently the goddess forgot her anger and smiled on him. So once more King Eurystheus, who had hoped to get Hercules into trouble, was disappointed.

For the fourth labor, the king now thought he had found something really dangerous. He ordered Hercules to bring in the Erymanthian Boar alive. To overcome the savage beast at all seemed difficult to him, but to drag it all the way back to the city of Mycenae, still alive and struggling, was quite impossible, the king thought. He rubbed his hands with particular satisfaction as he sent Hercules off on this errand. And for many a night he was joyful at the feastings as he drank his wine and pondered over his enemy's death.

Hercules sought out the Erymanthian Boar in its lair and attacked it with spear and club till it fled before him. He drove it up the mountainside until he forced it into a deep snowdrift where it plunged till it was quite exhausted. He picked the brute up, slung it over his back upside down, and carried it, struggling and gnashing its great tusks, all the way back to Mycenae.

15

Presently to King Eurystheus came the news that Hercules was arriving. Up he went to the walls of Mycenae and saw him in the distance bent under the weight of the vast, black, savage monster, which was plainly very much alive. It began to dawn on King Eurystheus that this time he had been a bit too clever. Hercules was going to put that dreadful beast down right in front of him. It was going to tear like a thunderbolt straight at the nearest man, and he would certainly be the nearest man. King Eurystheus went deadly pale. He raced back to his palace as fast as his trembling legs would carry him. But he wasn't safe there. Already he could hear the shouts and cheering as Hercules came through the city gate.

In another minute or two he would be at the palace steps. Eurystheus tore through the great hall down into the cool, dark storage room at the back. There his eye fell on the huge water jars, half buried in the ground, which slaves filled every morning before the sun got hot. One of them was already empty. Happy thought!

King Eurystheus clambered over the edge, slid into the cool, slimy inside, and pulled the lid over him with a bang. There they found him some hours later, still white and terrified, so that even his own servants had to smile. They could not resist teasing him with the announcement that Hercules was looking for him to present him with his boar.

4. FIFTH, SIXTH, AND SEVENTH LABORS

KING EURYSTHEUS had made himself ridiculous. Now he was even angrier than before. The first thing he did was to make a rule that in the future Hercules should deliver his prizes not to himself but to the officials at the city gate. All the same he was at a loss for a fifth labor, since he could not think of anything which would be dangerous to the man who could bring home alive on his shoulders the Erymanthian Boar. This time he simply determined to be insulting. He ordered Hercules to go and clean out the stables of King Augeas in a single day.

Hercules was unable to refuse this command, but he thought he would get the better of Eurystheus none the less. His first move was to go to King Augeas and, without revealing that he had been commanded to do it, offer to clean out his stables singlehanded for a great reward. King Augeas could hardly believe his

17

ears. He was certain the task could not be done. Therefore he was willing to promise anything. The two made
a bargain, and then Hercules went off to look over the
stables for himself.

The herds of Augeas pastured around two rivers,
and his stables were built where these flowed together.
There were pens for sheep and pens for cattle, many
pens for each because Augeas had countless herds.
Hercules stood by them in the evening and watched the
beasts come home. First came the sheep in enormous
flocks with men behind them and dogs running hither
and thither on either side. The whole meadow was
covered with huddled, fleecy backs, and their baaing filled the air. Then came the cattle, herd on lowing
herd, till the ground around the stables was all churned
into mud. With the cows went three hundred white
bulls and two hundred red. A small army of herdsmen
fastened wooden guards about the feet of the cows
that were to be milked, another group let the calves
in to their mothers, some milked or carried pails.
Everywhere the sound of lowing and bleating arose
upon the evening air.

Augeas walked among his herdsmen, delighting in
the bustle of it all. Many as were his cattle, he knew
them all and would stop to discuss his favorites with

his herdsmen. Hercules went with the king, marking the vast cattle pens and the incredible quantities of dung that were accumulating there. Now he could readily see that it was quite impossible for one man to carry it all out. Yet as he looked at the low-lying plain and the rivers running through it, a trick came into his mind which would outwit both King Augeas and King Eurystheus. For not only would it clear the Augean stables in a single day, but it would not force Hercules to degrade himself by lifting a single basket of dung.

Early in the morning Hercules was out by the stables, watching the herds depart. As soon as they were gone, he started digging a great ditch from the beds of the two rivers to the stables. Then working with might and main he damned the streams, lifting up huge logs singlehanded and using vast rocks that no one else could carry. By midday the water was overflowing its banks and beginning to trickle into the ditch. An hour later it was flowing in a torrent into the stables of Augeas and clear across them, back into the stream bed lower down. In a few hours the rush of water had rolled all the dirt away. Hercules knocked down his own dams and blocked up his trenches, and by the time the herds came home at sunset, their whole yard was clean.

Augeas was furious. He had never intended to pay Hercules. It had never occurred to him that the question of payment would arise. Moreover, somebody had just told him that Hercules would have cleaned his stables for nothing, since Eurystheus had ordered him to do so. Augeas tried to deny his promise, and when witnesses agreed he had made it, he openly refused to keep it. He forced both Hercules and his own son, who supported the hero, to leave his kingdom.

The sixth task given to Hercules was to chase away the birds which infested the Stymphalian lake. These birds had great claws of shining brass, sharp curving beaks, and bronze feathers which they could loosen and send spinning through the air from an immense height, and which came down sharp end foremost, with the force of arrows. They preyed on all living things within their reach, killing and carrying off lambs and calves, and even young children. No man had been able to shoot with force enough to hurt them, but now Hercules took his bow, which none but he could bend, and his arrows, from which a scratch meant death, to see what he could do against these fierce creatures.

At first sight it looked as though his task might be difficult. The birds were nesting among the reeds at the end of the land, and it was hard to come at them or to see how many there were. Hercules took a great, bronze shield with which to cover himself from the deadly feathers, and huge bronze cymbals with which to make a noise. Then, planting himself on a rocky headland which overlooked the lake, he clashed and clanged with all his might till the birds flew up in great flocks from the reedy marsh below. Then, protected by his shield, he aimed his arrows and shot them down one by one. The distant hills re-echoed with the clang of the falling feathers and the harsh cries of the angry birds. They darkened the sky over him like a cloud, and the bolts fell thick as rain. But still the hero crouched safe beneath his shield and, one by one, loosed his arrows that never missed their mark. At last the remaining birds wheeled round and fled away to the island of Ares far out in the unexplored sea, and the lake of Stymphalus was deserted.

When Hercules returned from the Stymphalian lake, Eurystheus sent him off to the land of Crete for his seventh labor. His task there was to capture the Cretan bull. Eurystheus did this as a favor to King Minos.

King Minos ruled over a great sea empire. He was

therefore especially devoted to the sea god Poseidon. Many times he had made sacrifices to the sea god, yet still he felt that he had paid him insufficient honor. At last he planned a great procession but none of his possessions seemed a glorious enough offering. He went down to the sea, therefore, and prayed to Poseidon himself to send something more perfect than had ever yet been seen that men might talk of Poseidon's festival for generations to come. The great waves crashed on the beach in answer to his prayer, and from the foam there sprang up to the land a snow-white bull.

It was the most marvelous bull that anyone had yet beheld. Even the herds of Augeas held no such bull as this. It was huge, taller by two handbreadths than the largest of its kind. Its hair was white and curly, dazzling in the sun. Its horns were silvery as the water whence it had sprung, and its great, mild eyes were the deep blue of the sea.

King Minos had vast herds and was proud of them, but never had he seen such a bull as this. He thought of the snow-white cattle he could breed from it. He remembered his promise to Poseidon to slaughter this beast, and his heart was torn. Then the beautiful animal came up and nuzzled at his shoulder. He put an arm around its neck and felt the great, soft coat. He touched the silvery horns, and he simply could not bear to kill it. The festival took place next day with a lesser bull walking in the procession as the sacrifice. But the occasion was remembered none the less, for at the very moment of the sacrifice, men came tearing up to Minos disheveled and gasping.

"The bull!" they panted, "the bull!" And for a moment that was all they could say.

"How dare you disturb the sacrifice?" asked Minos angrily. "The bull can wait."

"It is the bull from the sea," said one who had got his breath a little. "Suddenly he went mad. As we were guarding the cattle, he went mad and came down upon us. Six men are dead, King Minos, and all your cattle are scattered. For the rest of us, we fled as best we could and left him bellowing and gouging at the grass in savage fury on an empty plain."

From that time until Hercules' arrival, the white bull roamed the island, and no man's life was safe. Hercules could hardly persuade men to guide him to a grassy meadow where the bull was often seen. However, he faced the creature there at last and stood to await its charge. When it came, he stepped lightly to one side. He seized the animal by a silvery horn and twisted by main strength until the bull was forced to turn towards him. Then he grasped both horns and twisted again until it bellowed with pain and sank to its knees.

For a long time the bull sought to toss its head and shake the hero off, or to lunge forward to impale him. At last, however, it saw that it had met its master and turned to the hero as gently as it had turned to Minos when it first came out of the sea. Hercules took the bull back to Eurystheus, but he did not give him to the king. He merely showed him at Mycenae and then let him go.

5. EIGHTH, NINTH, AND TENTH LABORS

THE EIGHTH LABOR that Eurystheus gave to Hercules was to fetch the mares of Diomede. To the north of Greece lay the savage land of Thrace. It was a country famous for its horses and war chariots, but the mares of King Diomede were the fiercest and swiftest of them all. No man but their driver could be trusted with them. There were rumors too that Diomede fed them on human flesh.

Hercules found that this horrible tale was perfectly true as he burst into the stables by main force in spite of the resistance of the grooms. Remains of the dreadful food were still in the mangers, and the mares were chained and hobbled to prevent them from killing the grooms. They turned on him with bared teeth as he broke the links that held them to the manger, but he seized each one by the mane and forced their heads apart. Then Hercules led them out still shackled and trying their best to plunge and rear, but helpless in his grip. The stable hands, who had felt his strength when they tried to prevent him from entering, dared not raise hand against him, but stood by and watched him go. Hercules might have got off unmolested if the huge Diomede had not made after him. With a roar of rage he rushed at Hercules, who seized him round the waist and hurled him headlong. Unfortunately Diomede fell at the feet of his own mares, and that was the end of him.

Hercules gave these mares as a present to Eurystheus. He must have thought that such a gift would embarrass the cowardly king. Soon after the mares did burst out of their stables and escape. But they did no harm. They went to the woods of Mount Olympus, and there wild beasts devoured them.

By now Eurystheus despaired of destroying Hercules. All he could think of was to get him away for a long, long time. For the ninth labor, therefore, he sent him to fetch the belt of Hippolyte, who was queen of the far distant Amazons.

The Amazons were a nation of women, great archers, and fighters. They visited their husbands in another country and they sent their male children there. The females they reared themselves and taught them how to fight so fiercely that all the neighboring lands were afraid of them. The shimmering belt of Hippolyte, which was the token of her authority, had been given her by the war god Ares. Eurystheus hoped that to fight with a whole nation for the precious belt would be beyond even Hercules' powers.

For this ninth labor Hercules needed a ship and a crew of warriors. He sent out messages to all the lands of Greece for volunteers. Soon men came flocking eagerly to join him. Hercules set forth with his comrades and sailed across the sea to the northeast. He and his friends had many adventures on the way, for the journey was long and as perilous as Eurystheus had hoped. As always, however, everything Hercules did only served to increase his reputation. When he came to the land of the Amazons, it seemed at first as though he

were going to have no trouble at all. For the queen of the warrior Amazons loved bravery, whether in man or woman, and when she heard of Hercules' arrival, she came in person down to his ship to visit him.

Hercules greeted her royally and told her why he had come. And at that the queen laughed and gave him the belt, saying: "Ares himself gave me this belt because, though a woman, my whole soul is set on deeds of daring and heroism in war. With what better gift could I honor the hero whom all Greece declares the greatest of mankind?"

Hercules thanked the queen for her gift, and the two talked together in friendship, telling each other stories of the great deeds they had seen and done. As they sat together, a mob of yelling Amazons came sweeping down onto the beach. The queen's guard of honor, who had escorted her to the shore, had seen her take off the flashing belt and hand it to Hercules as she stood on the deck of the ship. Instantly the word went around among them that the queen had been made a prisoner. Some stayed to watch and wait while a group sped off to the city to arouse the others. Now they came like a swarm of angry bees. Some rained arrows on the ship from behind the sand dunes; others swam out through the shallow water and swarmed up the anchor ropes. The sea was alive with Amazons. They caught at the oar-holes and pulled themselves over the side. They leaped on the deck, fierce and nimble as tigers. They fell on the men like furies, without thought for their own lives.

There was no chance to explain. One moment all was peaceful; in the next there was utter confusion. The men grabbed their own weapons and resisted as best they could. In the end it was the presence of Hercules that turned the scale. Outnumbered though his men were, with his irresistible strength on their side they had the advantage. He seemed all over the deck at once, and with every blow an Amazon lay dead. At last the attackers saw they were defeated. They fled in dismay, leaving the deck strewn with corpses, among which lay the body of Hippolyte.

In the confusion the queen herself, the innocent cause of the battle, had been killed. Hercules sailed away with the belt and brought it to Eurystheus. But he sorrowed for the death of the brave queen who had given him her friendship.

Having sent Hercules to the east to face the dangers there, Eurystheus now determined to send him to the west. Accordingly he ordered him for the tenth labor to fetch the cattle of Geryon from Gadira, which is now the Spanish port of Cadiz. Geryon was a vast monster who was one man from the waist down but three from the waist up. He had three heads and six arms, while his strength was also that of three, so that he was famed to be the strongest of mankind. As for Gadira, it was out on the great ocean which was the border of the known world. Far as he had been at the commands of Eurystheus, Hercules had never been as far as this.

This time Hercules took ship for Crete and thence to Egypt and traveled all across North Africa to the strait which divides it from Spain. On the way he performed great feats wherever he went. Men said he cleared Crete of wild beasts, conquered Egypt, killed all the wild beasts which infested North Africa, and came at last to the narrow sea which divides North Africa and Spain. Here Hercules stood on the very edge of the world. To commemorate his journey he set up two immense rocks, one on each side of the strait. There the hills stand to this day on either side of the seaway between the Mediterranean and the Atlantic. The most famous of them is now named Gibraltar, but the Greeks called both the Pillars of Hercules.

From the Pillars of Hercules, the hero embarked on the vast Atlantic Ocean which the Greeks called part

GREEK MYTHS

of the River of Ocean that they thought ran round the edge of the world. Some say that the sun god himself gave him a golden cup, huge as a boat, and that he set out in that on the deep, mysterious sea. For he bent his bow at the sun in anger at the heat of the African shore, and the sun god laughed at his daring and aided him. Then the god Oceanus himself, on whose river the hero was journeying, was angry at the impertinence of the mortal who dared sail his great waters. He raised a huge storm, and the magic cup rocked wildly amid the boiling spray. At last Hercules saw the distant figure of old Oceanus, his long white beard streaming over the waters, and aimed an arrow at him. Then Oceanus too laughed and allowed him to proceed.

Hercules landed close by Gadira and came on the red cattle of Geryon grazing in a green meadow. Immediately he was attacked by Geryon's great two-headed dog, which came at him snarling, leaping straight for his throat. With a single blow of his club Hercules laid the monster low and returned to face Geryon's savage herdsman, who was also attacking him. He too fell before Hercules' club. The hero herded the wild cattle together, with some difficulty for they were very wild, and started to drive them off.

At that up came the monster Geryon, striding along with a tread that shook the ground. His three heads bristled with rage, his three mouths roared threats, and each of his six arms brandished a mighty club. Eurystheus had sent Hercules out hoping that here at last he would meet his match. Geryon certainly looked dangerous, but for once Hercules did not stop to wrestle with him. Instead he laid him low with a deadly arrow, drove the herd into his magic cup, and set out with them for the Pillars of Hercules.

From there, however, he drove the cattle all the way back by land, up through Spain, round the sea to Italy, and thence overland to Greece. Once people tried to steal the cattle. Once they were scattered in the mountains by a plague of stinging flies. One bull swam across the straits to Sicily, and Hercules had to go over and bring it back. Some he lost completely. Nevertheless, he brought most of the herd safely back to King Eurystheus.

6. ELEVENTH AND TWELFTH LABORS

THE ELEVENTH LABOR imposed upon Hercules was to fetch the apples of the Hesperides. Long ago at the wedding of Zeus and Hera, all things had brought presents to the bride. The gift of Earth had been trees with golden apples, shining like stars but sweet and scented as other apples are. They were a marvel among all fruits, the fairest that had ever been seen.

When the goddess Hera saw these, she loved them more than all her other gifts, and had them planted in the garden of the gods. This was a lovely garden full of green meadows and golden daffodils. Here grew all the flowers the gods delight in: roses, violets, narcissus, and many others, all larger and fairer than those growing elsewhere in the world. There were tall, green trees, arbors of trailing vines, white blossoming pear trees, dark cherries, and every kind of fruit. The nymphs who dwelt by its bubbling streams were called Hesperides. Since they cared for the garden, it was often called the Garden of Hesperides.

But delightful as was the garden, nothing in it had ever yet been seen so fair as the golden apples of Hera. Presently, therefore, Hera sent a dragon there to help the nymphs guard the treasure, which Eurystheus now ordered Hercules to steal.

It happened that while men knew about this garden, the apples, and the dragon, no one knew for a certainty where the garden was to be found. It was a secret retreat for the pleasure of the gods into which men might not come. Hercules had to set forth, he knew not whither, asking all he came upon if they had heard of the garden. At last he came to the river Eridanus, which is now called the Po. There he saw the white river nymphs in their silvery garments playing on the broad, blue stream. He called to them, saying, "Tell me, daughters of Zeus, where lies the Garden of the Hesperides?"

The river nymphs ceased their rippling laughter and looked at him suspiciously, ready to dart away like fish into the bottom of the stream. But the eldest of the nymphs recognized the hero by his club and lion skin and answered him fearlessly.

"We only know that we do not pass that garden as we ride down our hurrying stream from the mountains to the sea. Ask the wise sea god Nereus, for he is very old, and the ocean, touching all lands, beholds many things. He knows the garden if you can make him tell."

"But how shall I find Nereus?" Hercules answered her. "I cannot pursue a sea god into the ocean's depths. "How shall I make him tell."

"There is a little cove," said the eldest nymph, "which we see when we swim out into the ocean where the fresh water mingles with the salt. There old Nereus comes when the tide is low to sleep on a cushion of sea-weed in the bright rays of the sun. Hide there and watch him; then steal up and seize him while he sleeps. When he wakes and finds you have caught him, he will change himself into many different shapes, since he is as hard to grasp as water. Yet hold him fast, for when at last he sees that he is captured, he will tell you all you wish." She was gone with her sisters in a silvery flash, and only a ripple lingered on the surface of the stream.

Down near the mouth of the river Hercules found the rocky cove. While the tide was yet high he hid himself there to wait the slow hours till it went down. At last when the wet rocks and little pools lay uncov-ered in the sun, he saw snow-white sea gulls wheeling and turning over a great wave coming in from the sea. The wave reared up and broke in a green wall, and out of the foam rose a little, bent old man. Water dripped from his fingers and the ends of his long, white hair. Shells and seaweed hung in his locks; green ooze covered his garments. He came puffing slowly up be-tween the rocks, but his sea-blue eyes were bright and keen.

At length he came to a low, flat rock, sloping gently from the edge of a little pool. There he laid himself

down on the seaweed cushion, and the gulls flew silently round him for fear of disturbing him. Then he slept, his feet half in clear water, while the sea anemones waved beneath them and the crabs and starfish climbed idly around. Presently he snorted like a great old sea lion, until the whole cove resounded with his breathing. A smell of fish arose in the warm air.

Hercules crept from his hiding and seized the old man in his mighty arms. Quick as a flash the blue eyes opened, the old limbs twitched. In a moment the god was gone and Hercules found himself plunged to the shoulders in a raging fire. For a second his grip relaxed, and then, for the fire did not burn, he clutched more tightly than ever at what he could feel, though he did not see.

The form changed under his hands to a leaping stag, and he caught the animal to his breast just as it was jumping free. It shrank in his arms to a screaming sea gull which pecked at his eyes and struggled to get loose. He crushed it tight against him. In the instant it was a raging lion. He seized it by the neck and held it at arm's length away from him, but it changed to water and ran through his fingers in the twinkling of an eye. He hurled himself at the little pool, falling headlong on top of it, and it became a coiling snake, wriggling from underneath. This he seized by the neck and squeezed savagely, and with that the god gave in, and Hercules found himself lying on top of the old man himself with his fingers on his throat.

Then old Nereus, seeing that there was no escape, gave Hercules the answer he wished to know. "Go to the mountains of Atlas," he said, "where that giant stands, supporting on his shoulders the blue bowl of the sky. Ask him about the Hesperides, for they are his daughters, and at his bidding they will give the apples to you."

Hercules released the sea god and set out once more. At the end of his journey he came to the mighty giant, standing bowed beneath the great weight of the sky.

"Yes, I know the garden," Atlas answered the hero, "but you can never enter there. It is the special garden of the gods themselves; no mortal man has ever set foot in it. Do but hold up the weight of the sky for me, and I will fetch the apples that Eurystheus asks of you."

Hercules bowed his back to receive the monstrous weight, and the giant slipped away from under it and set out for the Hesperides. It seemed a long wait to Hercules. Even his mighty muscles were cracking beneath the strain when at length the giant returned with three of the gleaming apples in his hand. "Stay here," he said happily to the hero. "For many ages I have cramped my muscles beneath this load. Now it is your turn. I will take the apples to Eurystheus and tell him you sent them."

Hercules glanced at Atlas in dismay, but the giant was quite in earnest. Hercules was dreadfully afraid that he would never be released from his burden, but he thought of a trick, and pretending willingness, he said: "It is indeed my turn, and I should be glad to bear the burden for you for a little while. Why should I run across the earth at the commands of King Eurystheus? Take him the apples and tell him I cannot come. Nevertheless, before you go, take the weight for a little, while I fold my lionskin into a pad for my shoulders."

The simple-minded giant took up the burden again and released Hercules, who did not stay to help him further. He took the apples and at once set off for Greece.

This was the eleventh labor of Hercules, and for the twelfth, Eurystheus thought of the most terrible thing of all. He bade Hercules go down into the land of the dead and bring up Cerberus, the three-headed dog who watches at Hades' gate. He hoped, of course, that Hercules would be lost forever, as Theseus had been lost—that the powers of the underworld would be strong enough to keep him imprisoned. But Hercules simply shouldered his club and made off down the long, dark, winding road to the gray banks of the Styx and the shadowy towers which guard the lands of the dead.

He took no gifts for the ferryman as Psyche had, nor had he the magic voice of Orpheus to move the listening ghosts to tears. Yet he strode through the waiting shades unafraid and faced old Charon with such boldness that the grim, red-eyed ferryman shrank from him and let him stride unmolested into his muddy barge. Thus Hercules crossed the wailing river, while the barge sank low in the water at the weight of a living man.

At the gate of Hades sat the three-headed dog, its eyes as huge as saucers and its grinning teeth as fierce as those of a great lion. When it saw the huge hero advancing on him in the midst of the pale throngs of ghosts, the snarling died away in its three throats and it crouched before him. For the moment Hercules passed it by and came through the gates into Hades' house. There from the dark anteroom came a cry, and Hercules saw his friend Theseus imprisoned in a huge chair of stone. Theseus had come down safely to Hades, living man though he was, but when he came to the house of Hades he sat down when invited on this magic chair. Then the chair held him fast, and for all his strength he might have sat there forever if Hercules had not burst his bonds for him.

Hercules strode into the dark hall where gray Hades sat beside the pale Persephone, and asked them if he might carry Cerberus up to the daylight. He did not do this of his own will, he said, but by command of King Eurystheus, and when he had brought him the dog, he would let it go again.

The grave Hades nodded, and sad Persephone smiled on him, but neither said a word. Thereupon Hercules strode out to Cerberus and grasped him as he lay crouched in the shadow of the gate. At that the monster howled with a deadly howl such as the underworld had never heard before, and the three dog's heads gnashed and tore at Hercules, while the serpent that was its tail wound round his limbs. But Hercules held him so tightly that the heads were half strangled and could not get a grip except on the lionskin which partly protected him. For all the pain, Hercules hung on, throttling harder, till the snarling died away into muffled growls and the jaws relaxed. Then he heaved the animal over his shoulder and carried him up, the three hideous heads lying limply by his own, and the huge length trailing behind him on the rocky ground.

The road was steep, yet his strength never failed. All the way up to the world he carried him, and staggered out into the light. He reeled across the plain to Mycenae, keeping his strangling grip on the beast, for he dared not for an instant let go. When he came to the city gate where he should show his prize, the judges fled in dismay before him, and he stalked through the gate unmolested and himself laid the hideous beast at King Eurystheus' feet.

Eurystheus was almost terrified out of his wits by Cerberus. He had never intended to see him at all, and only by the flight of his guards had he been exposed to him. Nevertheless he was forced to admit that Hercules' labors were fairly ended. He could only revenge himself by driving the hero out of the city, ordering him never to return.

The
Fateful Contest

ARACHNE was a maiden who became famous throughout Greece, though she was neither wellborn nor beautiful and came from no great city. She lived in an obscure little village, and her father was a humble dyer of wool. In this he was very skillful, producing many varied shades. Above all he was famous for the clear, bright scarlet which is made from shellfish, and which was the most glorious of all the colors used in ancient Greece.

Even more skillful than her father was Arachne. It

was her task to spin the fleecy wool into a fine, soft thread and to weave it into cloth on the high, standing loom within the cottage. Arachne was small and pale from much working. Her eyes were light and her hair was a dusty brown, yet she was quick and graceful. Her fingers, roughened as they were, went so fast that it was hard to follow their flickering movements. So soft and even was her thread, so fine her cloth, so gorgeous her embroidery, that soon her products were known all over Greece. No one had ever seen the like of them before.

At last Arachne's fame became so great that people used to come from far and wide to watch her working. Even the graceful nymphs would steal in from stream or forest and peep shyly through the dark doorway. They would watch in wonder the white arms of Arachne as she stood at the loom and threw the shuttle from hand to hand between the hanging threads, or drew out the long wool, fine as a hair, from the distaff as she sat spinning. "Surely Athene herself must have taught her," people would murmur to one another. "Who else could know the secret of such marvelous skill?"

Arachne was used to being wondered at. She was immensely proud of the skill that had brought so many to look on her. Praise was all she lived for, and it displeased her greatly that people should think anyone, even a goddess, could teach her anything. Therefore when she heard them murmur, she would stop her work and turn round indignantly to say, "With my own ten fingers I gained this skill, and by hard practice from early morning till night. I never had time to stand looking as you people do while another maiden worked. Nor if I had, would I give Athene credit because the girl was more skillful than I. As for Athene's weaving, how could there be finer cloth or more beautiful embroidery than mine? If Athene herself were to come down and compete with me, she could do no better than I."

One day when Arachne turned round with such words, an old woman answered her. She was a gray old woman, bent and very poor. She stood leaning on a staff and peering at Arachne amid the crowd of onlookers. "Reckless girl," she said, "how dare you claim to be equal to the immortal gods themselves? I am an old woman and have seen much. Take my advice and ask pardon of Athene for your words. Rest content with your fame of being the best spinner and weaver that mortal eyes have ever beheld."

"Stupid old woman," said Arachne indignantly, "who

gave you a right to speak in this way to me? It is easy
to see that you were never good for anything in your
day, or you would not come here in poverty and rags
to gaze at my skill. If Athene resents my words, let
her answer them herself. I have challenged her to a
contest, but she, of course, will not come. It is easy
for the gods to avoid matching their skill with that
of men."

At these words the old woman threw down her staff

and stood erect. The wondering onlookers saw her grow tall and fair and stand clad in long robes of dazzling white. They were terribly afraid as they realized that they stood in the presence of Athene herself.

Arachne herself flushed red for a moment. She had never really believed that the goddess would hear her. Before the group that was gathered there she would not give in; so pressing her pale lips together in obstinacy and pride, she led the goddess to one of the great looms and set herself before the other. Without a word both began to thread the long woolen strands that hang from the rollers, and between which the shuttle moves back and forth. Many skeins lay heaped beside them to use, bleached white, and gold, and scarlet, and other shades as varied as the rainbow. Arachne had never thought of giving credit for her success to her father's skill as a dyer, though in actual truth the colors were as remarkable as the cloth itself.

Soon there was no sound in the room but the breathing of the onlookers, the whirring of the shuttles, and the creaking of the wooden frames as each pressed the thread up into place or tightened the pegs by which the whole was held straight. The excited crowd in the doorway began to see that the skill of both in truth was very nearly equal. But, however the cloth might turn out, the goddess was the quicker of the two. A pattern of many pictures was growing on her loom. There was a border of twined branches of the olive, Athene's favorite tree, while in the middle, figures began to appear.

As they looked at the glowing colors, the spectators realized that Athene was weaving into her pattern a last warning to Arachne. The central figure in her design was the goddess herself competing with the sea god for possession of the city of Athens; but in the four corners were mortals who had tried to strive with gods and pictures of the awful fate that had overtaken them. The goddess finished before Arachne did, and stood back from her marvelous work to see what the maiden was doing.

Never before had Arachne been matched against anyone whose skill was equal to her own. As she stole glances from time to time at Athene and saw the goddess working swiftly, calmly, and always a little faster than herself, she became angry instead of frightened. An evil thought came into her head. Thus as Athene stepped back to watch Arachne finishing her work, she saw that the maiden had taken for her design a pattern of scenes which showed evil or unworthy actions of the gods. She showed how they had deceived fair

maidens, resorted to trickery, and appeared on earth
from time to time in the form of poor and humble
people.

When the goddess saw this insult glowing in bright
colors on Arachne's loom, she stepped forward, her
gray eyes blazing with anger, and tore Arachne's work
across. Then she struck Arachne across the face.
Arachne stood there a moment, struggling with anger,
fear, and pride. "I will not live under this insult," she

51

cried. Seizing a rope from the wall, she made a noose and would have hanged herself.

The goddess touched the rope and touched the maiden. "Live on, wicked girl," she said. "Live on and spin, both you and your descendants. When men look at you they may remember that it is not wise to strive with Athene." At that the body of Arachne shrivelled up. Her legs grew tiny, spindly, and distorted. There before the eyes of the spectators hung a little dusty brown spider on a slender thread.

All spiders descend from Arachne, the legend says. And as the Greeks watched them spinning their thread wonderfully fine, they remembered the contest with Athene and thought it was not right for even the best of men to claim they were the equal of the gods.

The Mysterious
Strangers

ONE TIME Zeus and Hermes came down to earth in human form. They traveled through a certain district, asking for food and shelter as they went. For a long time they found nothing but refusals from both rich and poor. Then at last they came to a little, one-room cottage where dwelled a poor old couple, Baucis and Philemon.

The two had little to offer. They lived entirely from the produce of their tiny plot of land and a few goats, fowl, and pigs. Nevertheless they promptly asked the

strangers in and set their best before them. The couch
that they pulled forward for their guests was roughly
put together from willow boughs. The cushions on
it were stuffed with straw. One table leg had to be
propped up with a piece of broken pot, but Baucis
scrubbed the top with fragrant mint and set some water
on the fire. Meanwhile her husband, Philemon, ran out
into the garden to fetch a cabbage. Then he lifted down
a piece of home-cured bacon from the blackened beam
where it hung. While these were cooking, Baucis set
out her best food on the table. There were ripe olives,
fresh onions and radishes, and eggs baked in the ashes
of the fire. There was a big earthenware bowl in the
midst of the table to mix their crude, homemade wine
with water.

The only other course was fruit, but there were nuts,
figs, grapes, and apples, for this was the harvest season of the year. Philemon also had in mind to kill
their only goose for dinner. The poor old man wore
himself out trying to catch that goose but somehow
the animal always got away from him. At last the
guests bade him let the goose be, saying they were
well served as it was. It was a good meal, and the old
couple kept pressing their guests to eat and drink. They

cared nothing that they were now using up in one day
what would ordinarily last them a week.

At last the wine sank low in the mixing bowl, and
Philemon rose to fetch some more. As he lifted the
wineskin he found to his astonishment that the bowl
was full. Then he knew the two strangers must be gods.
He and Baucis were awed and afraid. But the gods

smiled at them, and the younger one said, "Philemon, you have welcomed us beneath your roof this day when richer men refused us shelter. Be sure those shall be punished who would not help the wandering stranger. You shall have whatever reward you choose. Tell us what you will have."

The old man thought for a little with his eyes bent on the ground. Then he said: "We have lived together here for many years, happy even though the times have been hard. Never yet did we turn a stranger from our gate or seek a reward for entertaining him. In this small cottage, humble though it is, the gods have eaten. It is as unworthy of the honor as we are. If, therefore, you will do something for us, turn this cottage into a temple where the gods may always be served and where we may live out the remainder of our days in worship of them."

"You have spoken well," said Hermes, "and you shall have your wish. Yet is there not anything that you would desire for yourselves?"

Philemon thought again at this, stroking his straggly beard. He glanced at old Baucis with her thin, gray hair and her rough hands as she served at the table. "We have lived together for many years," he said again, "and in all that time there has never been a word of anger between us. Now, at last, we are growing old. Our long companionship is coming to an end. Grant us this one request. When we come to die, let us perish in the same hour and neither of us be left without the other."

He looked at Baucis. She nodded in approval, so the old couple turned their eyes on the gods.

"It shall be as you desire," said Hermes. "Few men would have made such a good and moderate request."

Thereafter the house became a temple. The neighbors, amazed at the change, came often to worship and left offerings for the support of the aged priest and priestess there. For many years Baucis and Philemon lived in peace, passing from old to extreme old age. At last, they were so old and bowed that it seemed they could only walk at all if they clutched one another. Still every evening they would shuffle a little way down the path that they might turn and look together at the beautiful little temple and praise the gods for the honor bestowed on them.

One evening it took them longer than ever to reach the usual spot. There they turned arm in arm to look back, thinking perhaps that it was the last time their limbs would support them so far. There as they stood, each one felt the other stiffen and change. They had time only to turn and say once, "Farewell," before they disappeared. In their place stood two tall trees growing closely side by side with branches interlaced. They seemed to nod and whisper to each other in the passing breeze.

The Beloved
Statue

PYGMALION was a sculptor, a worker in marble, bronze, and ivory. He was so young and handsome that the girls as they went past his workshop used to look in and admire him. They hoped that he would notice them. But Pygmalion was devoted only to his art. People seemed noisy and trivial to him, and ugly too. He had an image of beauty in his mind, and he worked over his statues from morning to night in search of a loveliness beyond his powers of expression. In truth, the statues of Pygmalion were far more beautiful than human beings. Each statue was more nearly perfect than the last. Still, in every one Pygmalion felt that there was something lacking. While others would stand entranced before them, he never cared to look on anything he had finished. Immediately he was absorbed in his next work.

At last, however, he was working on an ivory statue of a girl in which he seemed to have expressed exactly what he longed to show. Even before it was done, he would lay down the chisel and stare at his work for hours. By the time the statue was nearly finished, Pygmalion could think of nothing else. In his very dreams the statue of the girl haunted him. Then she seemed to wake up and come alive. This idea gave him exquisite pleasure, and he used to dwell on it. The dreams passed into day dreams until for many days Pygmalion made little progress on his almost-finished statue. He would sit gazing at the maiden, whom he had christened Galatea. He would imagine that he saw her move. What joy it would be if she actually were living! He became pale and exhausted; his dreams wore him out.

At last, the statue was finished. Half the night Pygmalion gazed at the beautiful image; then with a hopeless sigh he went to bed, pursued as ever by his dreams.

The next day he arose early, for he had something to do. This was the day of the festival of Aphrodite, the goddess of beauty, to whom Pygmalion had always felt a special devotion. Never once had he failed to give Aphrodite every possible honor that was due to her. His whole life was lived in worship of the goddess. Many splendid gifts were being given her today—snow-white bulls their horns covered with gold, wine, oil, and incense, embroidered garments, carving, offerings of gold and ivory. Both rich and poor came in turn to offer their gifts.

As he approached the altar, Pygmalion prayed earnestly. Suddenly he saw the fire that burned there leap into flame. Excitement stirred within him; he could stay no longer; he must get back to his statue, though he did not quite know why.

Galatea was as he had left her. He looked at her longingly once more. Again as so often before, Pygmalion seemed to see the statue stir. It could be only a trick of imagination, he knew. It had happened so many times before. Nevertheless, on a sudden impulse, Pygmalion went over to Galatea and took her in his arms.

The statue was moving! He felt the hard ivory grow soft and warm in his clasp. He saw the lips grow red and the cheeks blush faintly pink. Unbelieving, he took her hand and lifted it. He felt the fingers gently tighten in his own. Galatea opened her eyes and looked at him. There was understanding in her gaze. The red lips parted slightly. As Pygmalion kissed them, they pressed against his own. Galatea stepped down from her pedestal into Pygmalion's arms a living girl.

The next day two lovers went to pray at Aphrodite's shrine: Galatea thanking the goddess for the gift of life, Pygmalion that his prayers had been answered and his lifelong devotion to the goddess rewarded.

How the Seasons Came To Be

Demeter was the great earth mother and goddess of the harvest. Tall and majestic was her apperanace, and her hair was the color of ripe wheat. It was she who filled the ears with grain. In her honor white-robed women brought golden garlands of wheat as first fruits to the altar. Songs and feasting did her honor as the hard-working farmer gathered his abundant fruit. All the laws which the farmer knew came from her: the time for plowing, what land would best bear crops, which was fit for grapes, and which to leave

63

for pasture. She was a goddess whom men called the great mother because of her generosity in giving. Her own special daughter in the family of the gods was named Persephone.

Persephone was the spring maiden, young and full of joy. Sicily was her home, for it is a land where the spring is long and lovely, and where spring flowers are abundant. Here Persephone played with her maidens from day to day till the rocks and valleys rang with the sound of laughter, and gloomy Hades heard it as he sat on his throne in the dark land of the dead. Even his heart of stone was touched by her gay young beauty, so that he arose in his awful majesty and came up to Olympus to ask Zeus if he might have Persephone as his wife. Zeus bowed his head in agreement, and mighty Olympus thundered as he promised.

Thus it came about that as Persephone was gathering flowers with her maidens in the vale of Enna, a marvelous thing happened. Enna was a beautiful valley in whose meadows all the most lovely flowers of the year grew at the same season. There were wild roses, purple crocuses, sweet-scented violets, tall iris, rich narcissus, and white lilies. All these the girl was gathering, yet fair as they were, Persephone herself was fairer far.

As the maidens went picking and calling to one another across the blossoming meadow, it happened that Persephone strayed apart from the rest. Then as she looked a little ahead in the meadow, she suddenly beheld a marvelous thing. It was a flower so beautiful that none like it had ever been known. It seemed a kind of narcissus, purple and white, but from a single root there sprang a hundred blossoms, and at the sweet scent of it the very heavens and earth appeared to smile for joy.

Without calling to the others, Persephone sprang forward to be the first to pick the precious bloom. As she stretched out her hand, the earth opened in front of her, and she found herself caught in a stranger's arms. Persephone shrieked aloud and struggled, while the armful of flowers cascaded down to earth. However, the dark-eyed Hades was far stronger than she. He swept her into his golden chariot, took the reins of his coal-black horses, and was gone amid the rumbling sound of the closing earth before the other girls in the valley could even come in sight of the spot. When they did get there, nobody was visible. Only the roses and lilies of Persephone lay scattered in wild confusion over the grassy turf.

Bitter was the grief of Demeter when she heard the

news of her daughter's mysterious fate. Veiling herself with a dark cloud she sped, swift as a wild bird, over land and ocean for nine days, searching everywhere and asking all she met if they had seen her daughter. Neither gods nor men had seen her. Even the birds could give no tidings, and Demeter in despair turned to Phoebus Apollo, who sees all things from his chariot in the heavens.

"Yes, I have seen your daughter," said the god at last. "Hades has taken her with the consent of Zeus, that she may dwell in the land of mist and gloom as his queen."

When she heard this, Demeter fell into deep despair. She knew she could never rescue Persephone if Zeus and Hades had agreed. She did not care any more to enter the palace of Olympus where the gods live in joy and feasting. She took on the form of an old woman, worn but stately, and wandered about the earth, where there is much sorrow to be seen.

All the while that Demeter wandered, she gave no thought to her duties as the harvest goddess. Instead she was almost glad that others should suffer because she was suffering. In vain the oxen spent their strength in dragging the heavy plowshare through the soil. In vain did the sower with his bag of grain plant the even

handfuls of white barley. The greedy birds had a feast off the seed corn that season. If the corn did start to sprout, sun baked it and rains washed it away. Nothing would grow. As the gods looked down, they saw threatening the earth a famine such as never has been known. Even the offerings to the gods were neglected by despairing men who could no longer spare anything from their dwindling stores.

At last Zeus sent Iris, the rainbow, to seek out Demeter and appeal to her to save mankind. Dazzling Iris swept down from Olympus swift as a ray of light. She found Demeter sitting in her temple, the dark cloak still around her and her head bowed on her hand. Though Iris urged her with the messages of Zeus and offered beautiful gifts or whatever powers among the gods she chose, Demeter would not lift her head or listen. All she said was that she would neither set foot on Olympus nor let fruit grow on the earth until Persephone was restored to her from the kingdom of the dead.

At last Zeus saw that he must send Hermes of the golden sandals to bring back Persephone to the light. The messenger found dark-haired Hades sitting upon his throne with Persephone beside him, pale and sad. She had neither eaten nor drunk since she had been in the land of the dead. She sprang up with joy at the message of Hermes. The dark king looked gloomier than ever, for he really loved his queen. Though he could not disobey the command of Zeus, he was crafty, and he pressed Persephone to eat or drink with him as they parted. Persephone was eager to be gone, but the king entreated her to eat something. To avoid argument and delay, she took a pomegranate from him and ate seven of the seeds. Then Hermes took her with him, and she came out into the upper air.

When Demeter saw Hermes with her daughter, she started up, and Persephone too rushed forward with a glad cry and flung her arms about her mother's neck. For a long time the two caressed each other. At last Demeter began to question the girl. "Did you eat or drink anything with Hades?" she asked her daughter anxiously, and the girl replied:

"Nothing until Hermes released me. Then in my joy I took a pomegranate and ate seven of its seeds."

"Alas," said the goddess in dismay, "my daughter, what have you done? The Fates have said that if you ate anything in the land of shadow, you must return to Hades and rule with him as his queen. However, you ate not the whole pomegranate, but only seven of the seeds. For seven months of the year, therefore, you must dwell in the underworld, and the remaining five you may live with me."

Thus the Fates had decreed, and even Zeus could not alter their law. For seven months of every year Persephone is lost to Demeter and rules pale and sad over the dead. At this time Demeter mourns, trees shed their leaves, cold comes, and the earth lies still and dead. But when in the eighth month Persephone returns, her mother is glad and the earth rejoices. The wheat springs up, bright, fresh, and green in the plowland. Flowers unfold, birds sing, and young animals are born. Everywhere the heavens smile for joy or weep sudden showers of gladness upon the springing earth.

The Boy Who
Flew Too High

THE KING of the island of Crete was called Minos. He had a great fleet and power that extended far and wide. He was also a fierce tyrant. He forced the people of Athens to send him every year seven youths and seven maidens, whom he fed to a horrible monster that he owned. This animal was called the Minotaur and was a creature with the head of a bull and the body of a man. To keep this beast safe and to prevent his victims from escaping, it was necessary to build a special dwelling. For this purpose Minos hired a famous architect whose name was Daedalus. Daedalus built a maze for Minos, so elaborate in its windings that no man without a clue could possibly escape from it.

Minos was delighted with his labyrinth and held the builder in great honor. Unfortunately when the wandering artist wished to take his fee and go, the king had other ideas. There were many things that could well be made for him by the great craftsman, and he saw no reason why he should let the man build things for someone else. Being king over an island, Minos found it easy to keep Daedalus where he was. He simply forbade all ships to give the artist passage. Then he provided him with an elaborate workshop, and suggested that he might as well settle down and be happy.

Thus Minos gained the services of Daedalus. But the great artist was not content. Beyond anything else he loved freedom to wander as he pleased, seeing the world and picking up new ideas. He was not the kind of man who could easily settle down. When he saw that he could not possibly get away by ship, he turned his talents to working out some other way of escape.

Minos did not visit the fine workshop he had given his artist. If he had, he would have seen a curious sight. The whole place was deep in feathers. There were feathers of all shapes and sizes, some thrown down as they had been brought in, and some neatly sorted into heaps. The young boy, Icarus, Daedalus' only son and companion, was doing the sorting. Daedalus himself was busy with twine, wax, and glue, fixing the feathers together in orderly rows on a wooden framework.

Daedalus was making wings. He had seen that it would be impossible to cross the sea by boat because of Minos' order, so he had determined to fly across it. After studying the wings of birds for a long time, he designed wings which he thought would support a man. Now he was working on them. Icarus was terribly excited and was helping eagerly. He did not so much dislike living in Crete, but he wanted to fly as the gods do. Think of being the first man to have wings!

The wings took a long time to finish, but at last they were done, a mighty pair for Daedalus, and a smaller pair for his son. The workshop was in the top of a lofty tower so Daedalus planned that there they would launch themselves into the air. As they stood fastening the wings onto their shoulders, Daedalus gave his excited son some last instructions.

"I shall go first," he said, "to show the way. We must go straight across the sea by the shortest route, lest we become tired and drown before we can reach land. Follow me, and remember the wings on your shoulders

are not natural wings, like those of Cupid. If you fly too near the sea, the feathers will become wet and heavy, and you will drown; if you fly up into the air as the gods do, the wax will melt in the sun long before you reach Olympus. Then your wings will fall off and you will perish. Follow me as I go through the middle of the air, neither too high nor too low. So you will be safe."

Daedalus jumped, falling like a stone till the wind caught him and he steadied. Then he began to rise again as the wings beat steadily from his shoulders. He turned and beckoned Icarus. Then Icarus jumped. The fall was terrible; so was the sudden stop as his spread wings caught the air. Still, the boy had the presence of mind to work his arms as he had seen his father do, and pretty soon he was sailing ahead in long swoops over the sea.

Presently the boy began to play tricks in the air. His father flew steadily on, but it would be easy, Icarus thought, to catch up with him. Father was too old to enjoy this properly. The swoops were rather sickening, but climbing was wonderful. Up, up he went, like the lark, like the eagle, like the gods. His father called something, but the wind whistled the sound away. Icarus realized he ought to come down, but nobody had ever been up there before, except the gods. Perhaps the real difference between gods and men was that gods could fly!

Up, up Icarus went, soaring into the bright sun. In vain Daedalus called to him. The boy was only a black speck by now.

At last Icarus came down. He came down fast, much too fast. In another second Daedalus caught sight of the boy whirling headlong. The framework was still on his shoulders. But the feathers had all fallen off. As Daedalus had predicted, the hot sun had melted the wax. One moment Daedalus saw his son; then with a mighty splash Icarus hit the water and was gone.

Daedalus circled round over the sea, not daring to go too low lest his own wings become soaked. But not even a clutching hand broke the surface of the water.

The white foam hung on the water for a moment; then it too disappeared. Sadly, Daedalus flew on. He reached the land at last, white-faced and exhausted. But he would never use his wings again nor would he teach others how to make them. This he had learned: It was not right for man to seek to soar like the gods.

The Winning of
Atalanta

ATALANTA, the swift-running huntress, was famous
for her beauty and courage. She hunted in the wild
woods, and though many young men came to woo her,
she steadfastly refused to marry. She loved her wild
freedom and every suitor she counted as an enemy.
Her father was not of the same mind, however. For
a long time he vainly urged his daughter to marry. At
last, losing his patience, he insisted she make a choice
among her suitors. Atalanta could not refuse her father
directly, but she decided to outwit him if she could.

She therefore set up a racecourse in a grassy valley, and declared that any who wished to marry must first race with her. He who could outrun her should be her husband. But if she were the faster, the beaten man should die. By this means she hoped to avoid having any suitors at all. Yet if they did persist, she could rely on her speed to defeat them.

At first the challenge of Atalanta acted only as a stimulus to her suitors. There were plenty of young men ready to risk their lives for fame and for the winning of so beautiful a bride. Perhaps they hoped that she would not be so cruel as to carry out her threat. But after a time it was known that the swift and slender Atalanta ran like the very wind itself and always demanded the penalty of death when she was the winner. Fewer and fewer men then came to race with her. When a race was to be run spectators thronged the racecourse. They were drawn to see so desperate a struggle and to catch sight of so cruel a maiden. Among these there was small pity for the unfortunate suitors. People thought they were fools to challenge the girl when many other beautiful and far kinder maidens might be won.

Among these spectators one day came Hippomenes, despising in his heart both the men who ran in the contest and the worthless girl who caused death to so many. So he thought until he saw Atalanta running swift as a wild deer, hair fluttering behind her and breath coming easily between her parted lips. Behind her toiled another runner. He labored with all his strength, but Atalanta spared no glance for him. Even when he was led away, she only stood there, cheeks flushed and panting slightly, looking out on the wild wood which was her home.

Hippomenes had never seen anyone so beautiful. This was indeed a woman to die for! Die he very likely would if he raced with her, for he had watched her running and seen that she did put forth all her strength. Yet he made the challenge. When the girl came—as was her custom—and said a few words to discourage him from running, he thought she looked on him kindly and that the color came into her cheeks as she met his eyes. But for all these signs of favor, he knew she would not spare him. He went then to the temple of Aphrodite and prayed earnestly for her aid. The goddess of love and beauty had no sympathy for Atalanta, who worshipped the cold moon goddess, Artemis. She came, therefore, to Hippomenes when he called her, put something into his hand, and gave him counsel.

With this Hippomenes waited in confidence for the morning.

When the race began, Hippomenes shot a little ahead of Atalanta and made a great show of putting out all his strength. But soon he seemed to fail a little, and swift feet came up behind him. Then for a moment the two raced side by side. The girl glanced at her rival uneasily, and Hippomenes saw with joy that she was reluctant to pass him. Yet he knew that soon she would. He stumbled a little and seemed to fail, so that she would draw ahead. Then he smiled to himself as he watched her. She was easy and confident. She thought he was beaten and that she could play with him.

At that he drew forth one of the things the goddess had given him and threw it before Atalanta on the path. It was a golden apple, a miracle of a fruit which the goddess had plucked herself from a living tree. It rolled along in front of Atalanta, and the wonderful beauty of it tempted her. She must have it, and the man was failing; there was plenty of time. She stooped to pick it up, and in that minute Hippomenes passed her. Still he seemed to be laboring and failing, though actually he ran fast. Atalanta marveled that with the efforts he made his speed did not slacken, and she was sure that soon it must. Again she ran evenly after him, caught up with him and passed him though she did not wish to. Again a golden apple rolled before her on the path.

Atalanta was angry at the challenge of this second apple. She knew now that the man, poor runner that he

was, intended to win by trickery. She would accept his challenge and win all the same. His hoarse breath seemed louder and louder, and greater the effort with which he ran. Nevertheless as she picked up the second apple, he passed her again. Now Atalanta was angry with him and ran, swifter than the wild deer, like the woodland wind itself. She passed him like the flickering shadow of a leaf. The goal was now in sight, and for the last time Hippomenes threw a golden apple. As the maiden stooped for it, he cast all pretence to the winds and ran for his very life. In an instant Atalanta was after him. But now the goal was very near. If she had known that he was not really exhausted, she would never have dared to stoop for the third apple. One moment she was two paces behind, and the next her breath seemed almost in his hair. But the winning post was only a few yards ahead, and still the girl was half a pace behind. They seemed for one breathless second to race side by side. Then with a final effort Hippomenes touched the winning post an instant before Atalanta's outstretched hand.

Such was the winning of Atalanta. The story says that the bride in spite of her anger at being tricked was not unhappy he won. At all events, Hippomenes married her amid great rejoicing, thanks to Aphrodite, who had known that a woman would certainly be tempted by the gift of the three golden apples.

The Adventures of Theseus

I. THE YOUTH OF THESEUS

THE TWO Greek heroes, Hercules and Theseus, had many adventures, and were famous for their characters as much as for their achievements. Hercules was the outstanding example of physical strength and fitness. Theseus was the wise, just ruler. Each of them therefore stood for something which the Greeks greatly admired.

Theseus was brought up by his mother, Aethra, in

her father's palace in the little kingdom of Troezen. It was a quiet, pleasant household where the boy learned to associate kindness and justice with the office of a king. Aethra saw to it that he was educated in running, jumping, wrestling, throwing the discus and javelin, boxing, swordplay, and all the skills of a prince.

He was taught also to love poetry and music. Wandering minstrels came to the palace singing of the great deeds of old. At the same time they brought news of the world as it was then, of greater kingdoms less pleasantly ruled than Troezen, of lawlessness, robbery, injustice, and of the heroes of Theseus' own time who fought against these evils. Aethra encouraged her son to listen, for she said he was a great prince and must take thought for these things. Yet when the boy asked her of his father, she would tell him nothing. She always answered that he must be patient until the time came for him to learn the truth.

The years went by and the boy became a youth fired with ambition to be worthy of a great destiny. At last he went to his mother one birthday and said to her, "Mother, I am now a man. Tell me about my father, for I am old enough to seek him out and to take my place in the world."

Aethra looked at her son thoughtfully. She noted the

brown arms, the steady blue eyes, the upright carriage, and the slender, athletic form that had not yet come to its full strength. "Perhaps it is time," she said at last. "Come with me and we will see."

Mother and son walked together up a pleasant hill towards a little grove of trees. As they went, the quiet voice of Aethra spoke of the daily tasks of the household, just as though this were an ordinary day and she had nothing to tell her son. When they came to the summit, she showed him a great, gray stone lying flat on its side half buried in the clinging grass.

"Lift up that stone for me if you can," she said quietly.

Theseus bent down to the stone and strained at it with all his strength. First he tried it from one side and then from the other. Finally he stood up and wiped his brow for a moment while he had a look at it. Then he dug a little of the earth away with his fingers to get a bitter grip and tore at it till it seemed as though his back would break. He might just as well have tried to lift a mountain for all the success he had.

"Never mind, my son," said the gentle Aethra. "Next year we will try again." She walked back towards the palace with her arm in her son's, talking calmly of other things.

Next year when his birthday came, Theseus went up once more with his mother to lift the mighty stone. This time he stirred it a little from its bed, and had it not been sunk so deeply in the earth, he might have raised it.

"Never mind, my son," said Aethra once more. "We can wait another year."

This was his second failure. Theseus determined that the third time, come what would, he must lift the stone. All day long he was out-of-doors, running, wrestling, exercising, even helping his grandfather's servants harvest the grain, carrying the heavy baskets of grapes to the winepress, and doing whatever hard work he could find. Therefore, when they walked up the hill again, mother and son were silent. They knew the great day was come. Each felt glad and sorry for the parting that lay ahead.

They looked down from the hilltop at the harbor, the quiet town, the few miles of pasture and plowland, and the uplands of scrub and heather which made up the little kingdom of Troezen. Far off to the north lay purple lines of rocky hills, pathless, and dangerous, but near at hand it was early summer and everything was green. Theseus and his mother stood there for a moment, listening to the distant baaing of goats and the calls of children, while the birds sang in the branches above them, bees hummed in the grass, and the warm sunlight fell across the stone. Then Theseus strode quickly to the stone, got his fingers beneath, and with a mighty heave raised it first knee high, then to his shoulder, and with a final gasp rolled it clear over onto its back in triumph. Beneath the stone, kept safe in a little hollow that had been scooped out for them many years before, lay a pair of sandals and a sword.

Theseus gathered up the treasures and turned back to his mother. "The time is come," he said to her. "Now tell me who is the father who left these things for me."

"He is Aegeus, king of Athens," Aethra answered him.

"Aegeus, king of Athens!" cried Theseus in exultation. "Aegeus, the lover of justice, the protector of the weak!"

"He said good-bye to me on this hilltop," said Aethra. "He rolled aside the stone himself and hid the sword and sandals beneath. Then he told me that if our child should prove a daughter, I was to keep her and bring her up and marry her well. If we had a son, I was to take him to this stone when he was grown man and bid him roll it away. If he could not, I should keep him with me; but if he were strong enough, I should send him to Athens with the sandals and the sword that he might claim his inheritance."

"His inheritance," repeated Theseus softly. He slung the sword about him and with the sandals in his hand turned to his mother. "Let us go," said he.

"Yes, we will," answered Aethra, "and tomorrow we will fit out a ship for you that you may travel like a prince."

"No, not by sea," said Theseus. "I shall travel by land, and alone."

"Alone and by land!" said Aethra quickly. "No, that can never be. By land the route is almost pathless. It is savage and lawless; robbers and strange monsters haunt it. No man travels by land, at least not alone."

"That is how I shall go," said Theseus firmly. "Is not Athens the city of justice, the refuge of the weak? I will destroy these robbers and monsters who rule the land. Thus when I come to my father, my fame will come with me and he will know that I was a worthy son."

Aethra begged her son to be reasonable. Her old father added his prayers, but it was no use. The next day Theseus put on the sandals, took his sword, kissed his mother, and walked quietly out of the palace toward the hills.

Athens is many days' journey to the north of Troezen, and, as Aethra had said, the way was perilous. Theseus was at home in the open, and he had a friendly word for the people in town or cottage wherever he came. Yet the hills were wild and lawless. He never knew whether a stranger was a peaceful shepherd or one of the fierce robbers who held the whole countryside in terror.

One day a curious looking man stepped out of the wood onto the path in front of him in a lonely stretch of the road. He was immensely shaggy with matted hair and beard. His shoulders were enormous, and he carried a huge club bound with iron. Yet from the waist down he was tiny, with little, crooked legs. He came shuffling along the path calling out in a high, nasal voice to the noble young stranger to have pity on a poor cripple and give him money. Theseus let him come near, thinking him harmless. When the creature was within arm's length he reared up and struck a blow with the massive club which would have dashed Theseus' brains out if he had not been young and quick. As it was, the youth jumped aside just in time, and, as the man swayed for a moment overbalanced by the force of his own stroke, Theseus snatched out his father's sword and stabbed the robber to the heart. He put the sword back in its sheath, took up the great club as a trophy of his first fight, and walked on. At the next village there was great excitement when people saw him carrying the club. They crowded round to thank him and to tell him that the robber was named the Club Bearer and had terrorized innocent travelers for many years.

Theseus' next adventure was with a robber called Sinis, or the Pine Bender, because he bent down to earth the tops of two pine trees and tied his prisoners between them. Then he let go, and the trees sprang upright again with a terrific force, tearing the poor wretches apart. Sinis rushed at Theseus with a mighty weapon made from the trunk of a pine tree. But strong as he was, Theseus was stronger, and the iron-bound club was superior to the pine. The Pine Bender was vanquished and came to the miserable end he had often prepared for others.

Theseus traveled on. Now his fame spread before him far and wide until people came down to the way to meet him. They came both to speak with a great hero and to beg him to deliver them from trouble. Thus Theseus was persuaded to kill a great wild

boar which was laying waste the countryside. Then
he came upon the dreadful Sciron, who sat by the
road where it passed over a steep cliff by the sea and
forced all passers-by to wash his feet. As the trembling
victim was busy with his task, Sciron kicked out and
tumbled him backwards over the cliff onto the rocks
below. Theseus gave him, too, a dose of his own medi-
cine. Then he passed on to another place where he
killed a mighty wrestler by dashing him to the ground.

By now even in the remotest parts, people would
come to greet Theseus and thank him for rescuing
them. He was not surprised, therefore, when one evening a man stepped out onto the road in a lonely
spot and offered him shelter for the night. He was a
queer man, though; he was very tall and thin with a
pale face and pale eyes that were never still for a
second. He shuffled his feet and cracked his fingers.
Everything about him was jerky except his voice,
which was smooth as oil. "You do my poor home
honor," he kept on saying. "So great a hero! So poor
a shelter! Yet perhaps you are wise. Many great and
noble men have spent the night with me." He laughed,
not very loud but on and on, as though at a joke of
which he was never weary.

"Where is your house?" said Theseus shortly,

for he saw no point in laughing and he did not like the man. "Perhaps it is too far. I must be on my road at dawn."

"Ah no," said the strange man quickly. "It is not far. Just over the hill. In ten minutes, in five minutes if the noble hero is willing, we shall be at the door Just five minutes from the highway! Think how easy. Yet of all the noble strangers who have rested in my bed, not one has roused himself to be on the roadway in the dawning. So sound a sleep! And dreamless! It is a noble bed!" He laughed again and jerked a hand onto Theseus' arm above the elbow as if to guide him.The grip was surprisingly strong. The youth suffered himself to be hurried up a rocky path, for he thought he knew the man now from stories that he had heard, and he was anxious to see what he would do.

At last they came in sight of a mean hovel. "Come in, come in," said the stranger quickly, pulling a little harder at his arm. "Come and rest. Did I tell you I have a bed for you? You are very tall, yet my bed will fit you. Oh yes, it will fit!"

Theseus pulled his arm free and turned on the man in the doorway. "I have heard of you," he said quietly. "Your bed is a hard plank and narrow, and it needs no blankets. Yet all men exactly fit it, so they say, and when they are laid upon it, they sleep very soundly in death. Is not your name Procrustes?"

Procrustes turned upon him and grasped his arm again. "Better men than you," he cried, "have fitted my dreadful bed. For if a man be too short when he is laid thereon, I stretch him till he fits it. But if he be too long, I shorten him with the knife. Now you shall lie, my young hero, where so many better men have lain before. You are tall for my bed at present, but it will fit you yet."

With that he threw his arms about Theseus and made as though to lift him. But the hero burst the grip with a mighty heave and seized Procrustes by the waist. Then he lifted him to his shoulder and bore him struggling through the dark doorway. Accordingly as night fell, Theseus set forth once more upon his road in the dark, leaving Procrustes stretched upon the terrible bed which had fitted all other men and now at last fitted him.

2. THE ADVENTURE OF THE MINOTAUR

MEANWHILE at Athens the long reign of King Aegeus was coming to an inglorious end. The whole land was split by quarrels between Aegeus' cousins, who considered themselves his heirs, while the old king himself was completely under the sway of the witch, Medea. Even the common people were tired of Aegeus, for he had been defeated in war by King Minos of Crete, and the land was forced to pay a dreadful tribute every nine years.

Theseus did not wish to make any claim on the old king. He came instead as a mighty hero who happened to be traveling through Athens and asked the king to receive him as a guest. Theseus hoped that his likeness to his mother, Aethra, would cause the old man to recognize his son.

Aegeus agreed to receive the hero, since he could hardly refuse the request of such a famous man. But Medea, the enchantress, had learned who Theseus was. She had already whispered that the young man was a traitor who came to seize his throne. The feeble old king believed her. Medea smiled to herself. She knew that if Theseus were recognized by his father, her reign in Athens would be at an end.

A great crowd of people poured out to meet Theseus at the gates of the city. They escorted him with shouts and cheering to the palace of the king. They stood on tiptoe in the crowd, to get a glimpse of the hero's head as it towered above the rest. When even the palace servants ran out at last, the old king quivered with anger.

"He is indeed a traitor," he said to Medea. "He steals my very servants from before my eyes."

Medea smiled at him. "I will deal with him," she said. "Let us go out on the steps to welcome him. We will greet him with honor and bid him come in. When he enters the hall, do you sit him down and call for meat and wine. I myself will pour his wine for him; he shall drink from my golden cup. There are poisons I have especially brewed. Let him take but one sip that I shall pour for him, and he will never claim your throne."

The old king nodded feebly, for he was half crazed by her spells. "Do not fail with the poison," he quavered, "and now help me to the door."

They stood on the steps to greet the hero, the slender, dark-eyed sorceress, and the tottering old man leaning on her arm. Theseus turned from the witch in anger, but he looked his father in the face. The old man had forgotten Aethra; he did not know her son. He bade Theseus welcome formally and invited him within. But he gave no sign of recognition, and the hero followed him, wondering.

The traveler was bathed and dressed for feasting. Tables were set up within the hall. Meat was brought in by the servants. Wine and water were mixed in huge bowls. Each guest was brought a winecup of red earthenware on which a skillful artist had painted some deed of a hero of whom the minstrels sang. Medea would not let Theseus drink from his.

"You are guest of honor," she said. "You shall drink from gold, and a king's daughter shall serve you."

With that she fetched him wine in a curious golden cup such as the great artists of Crete had made. Theseus took the cup and turned to his father, for he had a mind to drink his health. The old king was looking at him in a fixed silence, while his fingers drummed nervously on the table. There was something so unpleasant about his stare that Theseus was startled, and the first hint of treachery came into his mind. He determined to test his father. Therefore he kept his left hand on the winecup. With his right hand he drew out his father's sword and made as though he would cut himself a portion of the meat with it. Seeing that sword, the king reached out startled. He snatched the winecup from Thesus' hand, and dashed it to the floor. Then he jumped up and flung his arms about the young man, calling him son. For her part, Medea, seeing her treachery was discovered and knowing that her reign was over, vanished from Athens and was seen no more.

Aegeus proudly acknowledged his son and named him his heir. The king's cousins were not pleased at this. They stirred up the common people against King Aegeus. It happened to be the time when the tribute to Minos became due. Seven youths and seven maidens were chosen by lot from among the people to go to Crete as a sacrifice to the dreadful monster, the Cretan Minotaur. What happened to them when they got there no one knew. No one who once went in had ever come out of the famous labyrinth that Daedalus had made for the beast to dwell in. Men could hear the distant bellowing of the monster in his lair, and it was supposed he ate up his victims. At any rate, because their children were chosen by lot for a dreadful fate, the people were furiously angry. So too was Theseus when he heard the tale.

"Why has no one dared to slay this Minotaur?" he asked King Aegeus. "This is no way to pay tribute. Let me go to Crete and put an end to it."

"No, my son," said King Aegeus terrified. "No one can slay the Minotaur. The young men are not allowed to take any weapons as they go into the labyrinth. Besides, the victims are chosen from the people, and you are not of the people; you are the king's son."

"All the more reason I should go," said Theseus. "I shall not wait to be chosen. I shall volunteer."

The king implored him with tears in his eyes. But Theseus was determined, and the people idolized him more than ever when they heard what he was to do. The ship made ready for the chosen victims was small and quite unarmed, as the terms of the treaty bade. She had a black sail of mourning, that all might know that she bore the tribute to King Minos and must be allowed to pass. This time Theseus bade them put in a white sail as well. "When we return," he said, "we shall come with open rejoicing as a free people should."

The ship put out from the bay and the weeping people watched it go. King Aegeus sat on the headland looking after it. There, he told his son, he should watch daily until the ship came home. But the chosen youths and maidens, encouraged by the cheerfulness of The-

seus, sang songs to cheer their journey across the sea. When they came to the great wharves of the town of Cnossos, they put on a bold face. Even the powerful ships of Minos did not dismay them, or the sight of his huge stone palace, or the crowds of townsfolk who came down to watch the tribute come to land.

Many a man felt pity as he saw the handsome youth at the head of the little group and heard that he was the king's only son and that he was a volunteer. There was talk of granting him a weapon that he might have a fair chance against the Minotaur, but King Minos would not hear of it. The challenge of Theseus only made him angry.

"How dare you come here in defiance?" he said to the young man. "Tomorrow we will throw you to the monster and we shall see what your boast is worth."

"I dare because the tribute is unjust," replied Theseus firmly. "Armed or unarmed I will fight your hideous bullman. If I prevail, I warn you, O Minos, that we Athenians are a free people and the tribute shall cease. If I die, I die; but the tribute is still unjust."

Some murmured admiration at his boldness, but King Minos stood up from his throne in wrath. "Take his sword," he ordered his guards, "and lock the victims in the dungeons over night. Tomorrow we will give you to the Minotaur, and after that the tribute will go on. The black-sailed ship shall return to Aegeus to tell him that he has no son. The Athenians need to remember that the sea is mine. Distant as they are, they must live in dread of my power!"

The guards closed in on the Athenians and took them down to the cold, dark dungeons. People watched them pityingly. They knew Theseus had no chance, yet they admired the handsome young man who spoke so boldly before them all. None pitied him so much, however, as the soft-hearted king's daughter, white-footed Ariadne. She had heard Theseus speak in the hall as she stood beside her father, her bright hair about her shoulders and a great crown flashing with jewels upon her head. In the dead of night she left her chamber and stole on silent feet down the long stone corridors toward the dungeons. Quietly she drew the great bolt, and went in.

She stood in the moonlight which fell through a small, high window. Theseus thought she was some goddess at first, for her white feet were bare on the stone, there was gleaming gold on her scarlet garment, and the bright crown was still on her head. She bade Theseus rise and come with her, making no sound. "I will give you a sword," she whispered softly, "with which you may fight the Minotaur fairly and slay him if you can."

She took his hand to guide him in the long, dark passages, and together they stole down many corridors, past many a darkened door. At last they reached a little room from which ran a passage dimly lighted. From here they heard echoing faintly a low, hoarse bellowing sound.

"Here is the Labyrinth," said Ariadne. "Far off in the center lies the Minotaur. Bend down your ear to listen while I whisper to you the secret of the Labyrinth. To return is not so easy. Many doors lead out from the center; yet only one will bring you here. Take this sword in your right hand and this ball of thread in your left. We will tie the end of it to a pillar and you may unwind it as you go. Then it will be easy to return as you gather in the thread."

She gave him the thread and the sword, and watched him out of sight. For a while she heard his footsteps moving round and round within. At times they stopped as though he stood puzzling before the maze of passages. Then they went on again, and presently they died away.

Ariadne stood there for a long time looking at the

shining thread across the floor and hearing the distant roaring which arose from the monster's lair. She heard when he reached the center, because the roar grew suddenly louder and went on and on. Then there fell a dead silence, and for a long while nothing happened. If Theseus were dead or wounded, she might wait till morning and he would never come. It seemed hours that she had been standing, and the stone floor was very cold.

At last she heard sounds. Then someone twitched the line. The sounds came louder and clearer, till Theseus emerged from the passage with the sword red in his hand.

"Why were you so long?" Ariadne whispered. "It must be nearly dawn."

"It is a dreadful monster," Theseus said in answer. He was still shaken by the sight of the horrible creature whom few living men had seen.

"Quickly, then!" she whispered. "We have not much time."

Hand in hand they stole down the long corridors again, roused the group from their dungeon, and sped down to the little ship which was moored beside the wharf. There were urgent explanations in whispers. Then the sailors scrambled over one another to hoist

the sail. Very quietly they cast off, and shipped oars as soon as they dared. Then they fled for their lives as the sky grew pale with the first light before the dawn.

All day long they raced away, fearing pursuit from the great ships of the Cretan fleet. They had put up the black sail in the dark that morning, but when some spoke of it and bade them hoist the white one, the sailors refused to take the time. Frantically they rowed till they were exhausted. They landed at last, worn out, on the island of Naxos, where they lay down to sleep. In the morning there was a false alarm of a sail on the horizon, and tumbling into their ship, they fled again. In vain Theseus called to them that Ariadne had been left sleeping on the beach. Even though they owed her their lives, the sailors did not care. They were mad to reach Athens and safety.

Ariadne slept without waking till the ship was far out to sea. Then she wandered for a long time up and down, calling vainly for Theseus and the men who had forsaken her. At last the god, Dionysus found her and persuaded her to come up to Olympus and be his bride. To proclaim to all people that she had done so, he took her crown and set it in the heavens, where each jewel became a star, and where it can still be seen.

Theseus' terrified crew still raced toward Athens with no thought in their heads but speed. At last they came within sight of the headland on which King Aegeus sat, looking out over the blue ocean day after day for tidings of his son. Now he saw the black-sailed ship. The king was in despair, for he remembered the white sail they had taken with them, the sail Theseus had said they would hoist if they came back in freedom and rejoicing. The poor old man thought he had nothing to live for and, even as the joyful Theseus looked eagerly at the land, Aegeus threw himself over the cliff to perish in the sea.

Thus Theseus came to his throne with mourning instead of rejoicing. Thereafter he reigned long, and his rule was a famous one. The Athenians told many stories of his justice, his kindness to the common people, and of the ways in which he made Athens great. They told how Theseus offered protection to people who had suffered injustice in other lands. Some even declare that he gave up the title of king, preferring to give power to the people. Later his tomb became a place of refuge for poor men and slaves and all who had suffered wrong. While they were there, no man could harm them. In this way the Athenians honored the memory of Theseus, hero, lover of justice and protector of the oppressed.